Reclaiming
Yourself

A Black Woman's Guide to
Navigating Work, Life and Your Inner Spirit

Lydia Payne-Johnson

Reclaiming Yourself

Published by Arragon Consulting, LLC, Herndon, VA 20170.

ISBN: 978-1-7371287-0-0 (paperback)

Contents

Dedication

This book is dedicated to my mother,
Beryl Gwendolyn Payne (Ibae).

I'm grateful that she taught her daughters
how to be fierce and fabulous.

INTRODUCTION:
The Work-Life Balance Myth

Women have been fed the notion of work-life balance for over 20 years. In the workplace, we have put our heads down, taken on heavy workloads and clocked long hours. At home, we juggle getting our children to school, playdates, birthday parties and soccer practice to keep our families and households in order. For African-American women, our quest differs from our White counterparts. If you're a single mother, like I was early in my career, it was more than a career; it was survival for my child and me.

Balance? What is that? The true smoke-and-mirrors about work-life balance is that the term assumes that a woman's professional persona is somehow separate and distinct from her personal life. In actuality, just below the surface of that professional woman veneer is who we truly are along with our personal issues, insecurities, worries, fears and vulnerabilities.

The coronavirus pandemic changed forever how and where we work. In particular, women had to quickly pivot to remote working due to unexpected health and safety restrictions. The pandemic created once-in-a-century health and economic impacts that required setting up workspaces in kitchens, bedrooms, basements, living rooms, and attics. For many, it meant sharing space with your spouse or significant other who, like yourself, was now working from home.

For parents, the new health and economic impacts also changed the family dynamic. With schools and daycare centers closed, the new normal for children was remote learning. Balancing work and ensuring that your children had conducive environments to study and have downtime was a major paradigm shift for households. An extra stress factor for women was virtual meetings. Unlike our male counterparts, women still needed to play dress up; sprucing up our appearance by putting on makeup and styling our hair to look more presentable.

Black women, in particular, have been disproportionately impacted by the pandemic. A September

2020 Opinion piece in the Washington Post highlighted that, "...*Black women sit squarely at the confluence of multiple systems of oppression, and [have] experienced a disproportionate loss of life and livelihood in the era of covid-*19."[1] Moreover, the authors found that "...almost half of Black households with children are headed by single women, and so must face issues of child care and virtual schooling on their own...with Black women spending three times as many hours per week caring for elderly or sick relative [compared to] White women."[2]

Finding the right balance mentally, physically and emotionally under pre-pandemic conditions was already a challenge. For Black women the stress was magnified. Our work-life was now combined to be life on steroids 24/7. We faced unemployment and the possibility of reduced income while struggling to cover household expenses, including rent and mortgage payments. For many, we also had the extra expense of purchasing Personal Protective Equipment (PPE) which became a new survival necessity.

It's enough that Black women were already struggling with work-life balance. Issues going on in our personal lives are indelibly intertwined with our professional lives despite our efforts to compartmentalize and keep them separated. Our work and life encroach on each other daily. And, with the onset of the pandemic, there was no reprieve.

When a stress factor is triggered, we react and, for some of us, we retreat. At the point that the balance tips too far into either personal or professional, you're no longer able to see yourself. You're unable to see how your words, actions or even inactions, may alter others' perceptions of you, hurt your career and, importantly, how productive you are at work and at home.

We need to acknowledge that for African-American women, work and life has always been indelibly connected. So, I'm advocating that you ditch the work-life balance quest. It's a myth. All the things that the so-called experts have told us about what makes up work-life balance are the things that African-American women have been doing for centuries. It's not new to us. Trying to compete with White women in that space is a distraction. In fact, they should be trying to emulate us!

Here are some key questions around work-life balance for African-American women that have neither been asked nor answered:

- Does achieving work-life balance advance your career?

- Does having work-life balance mean that the microaggressions and unconscious biases you face are eliminated?

- Does having work-life balance mean that you're also connected to your inner self?

In this book, I want to help you shift the paradigm away from the unachievable towards the achievable. Specifically, how to redirect your energies on ways that will help you focus on your priorities personally and professionally, as well as tune into your goals, your values and your true self.

The 5 Habits to Reclaiming Your Inner Spirit

B alancing the demands of your personal and pro-fessional goals are challenging. African-American women, in particular, tend to lose sight of priorities because everything feels urgent. Additionally, there's the extra layer of those annoying, insulting and stress-producing microaggressions and unconscious biases that White co-workers toss at you on a regular basis. In juggling these silent stress factors, we forget to make ourselves a priority. We lose sight of who we are, our accomplishments, our credentials, our strengths, as well as the people, places, and activities that bring us joy.

There are times we may second guess our skills and abilities while striving to advance our careers. Other times, we may question whether we are "good enough" as we measure ourselves against others in our work environments. Each time we experience a form of microaggression, or an unconscious bias, it has an impact on our confidence and self-worth. Black women also are targets for a host of "Isms": racism, ageism, sexism, to name a few. These silent stressors are real, make no mistake. They're distractions that over time have operated to shift your focus away from your true self.

I'm sharing the 5 personal habits that helped me reclaim my inner spirit and redirect my focus back to who I truly am on the inside. I hope that these habits will inspire you to do the same. Now, let's define habit. I am defining habit as a pattern of behaviors or practices that set you up for recurring success in your career and happiness in your life. Each section of this book is followed by a suggested affirmation and also space for you to journal your thoughts and feelings. More importantly, I wanted to share things that can be done at any time and in a format that you can carry with you anywhere.

Let's dive in.

"I found God in myself . . . and
I loved her fiercely."

— Ntozake Shange[3]

The 1st Habit for Reclaiming Your Inner Spirit

Have a daily affirmation

Before African-American women can contemplate the present challenges that permeate the workplace and the media, African-American women need to reconnect with their emotional center: the inner self. This includes connecting those components that contribute to who you are as a woman: your emotions, your passions, your family, your ancestors, your guides, your talents. I'm a strong advocate for women to embrace these connections. One way of doing so is through daily affirmations.

Affirmations are powerful tools that can help you stay centered daily. Affirmations, said silently in combination with breathing techniques, bring you back from the noise and many distractions that persists all around you. They keep you reminded about the who, what and why of you and your existence. Affirmations are also short gratitude statements. When you affirm, "*I am open to the happiness that is mine today,*" you're also acknowledging that there is another Presence/ Higher Power who says happiness is yours for the taking, if you claim it, and acknowledge that there is a greater force guiding you. Affirmations are one of the ways you love and accept yourself. I've used affirmations most of my life. There have been different ones depending on where my life and my head was at the time. Affirmations have been given to me. I've seen them on tee-shirts, on the sides of buildings, the Bible, picked them up from conference materials, radio and television shows, and many other sources.

For me, affirmations serve to help me set goals. I've used them to motivate me before a job interview, speaking engagements, and presentations. I've even used affirmations to bring me back from the edge of anger or deep sadness. Something as simple as "I can do this!" is an affirmation.

There's no right or wrong to affirmations. There's also no defined time of day that affirmations are to be said. There's merely the commitment on your part to incorporate affirmations in your life, every day.

You can also write your own affirmations and I encourage you to do so. Plus, there's no shortage of affirmation books, authors and other resources including, Iyanla Vanzant, Marianne Williamson, Anne Wilson Schaef, Melody Beatty, Deepak Chopra, Panache Desai, Mark Nepo, to name a few.

Use the space below to write down your favorite affirmations or create your own. Pick an affirmation you can recite to yourself on a daily basis. Take note of how you feel when reciting your affirmation to yourself. You will notice a shift in your mindset and perspective.

_____

_____

_____

"I have the power to   _____
create my world."[4]   _____

_____

_____

_____

_____

_____

_____

_____

_____

_____

_____

_____

Lydia Payne-Johnson

"Truth is simple. When someone tries to make it complex, they are trying to hold onto the power it brings."

— Cynthia and Miles Chauvin[5]

The 2nd Habit for Reclaiming Your Inner Spirit

Nurture the Seeds of Your Successes

When was the last time that you took an inventory of your gifts, talents, goals and accomplishments? You must acknowledge that you were born with a set of gifts and talents that are specific to you and will set you up for a unique contribution in the world. Are you mining and leveraging your gifts and talents to the fullest? Remember that who you were and what you accomplished by the time you were 25 years old is different from who you are (or will be) at 30, 40 or older.

Early in my career, I was a single mother raising a young son and living in New York City. I didn't have a car. My transportation was the subway and the bus. Mondays through Fridays was getting my son, Andre, ready for school, fixing breakfast, getting myself ready and out of the house to go to work in lower Manhattan. By the time he was 10, my son was a latchkey kid, which meant that he was on the honor system to get home as soon as school was over, let himself into the apartment and stay inside until I arrived home around 6pm. Back then, there weren't cell phones or even the internet. So, he had to call me at work using the landline phone. Once home, I was fixing dinner, making sure his homework was done, then off to bed. Each day, we'd repeat the cycle over again. Andre played Little League baseball. His games almost always started before I got off work and I usually caught his games in the last 2 innings. Many times, my sister Diane, who also lived in the Bronx, would get there as my proxy.

On the weekends, it was finding interesting things for us to do that fit within my then meager budget. Sometimes we'd spend the day at the Bronx Zoo. Labor Day weekend was an art show in Greenwich Village. We'd hop on the subway then wrap up the day in Washington Square Park to have ice cream cones and people watch. Other activities he and I would do together included going to the movies, roller skating and visiting relatives. One annual event was to go to see the Macy's Thanksgiving Day parade. It didn't matter how cold it was outside. We'd get up at 5 am, bundle up (Thanksgiving Day was always cold), hop on the subway, find a spot in the crowd along Central Park West and watch the bands, floats and balloons. Once the parade was over, we'd head home on the subway. At home, we'd have hot chocolate and I always found a way to make Thanksgiving dinner. Overall, we had a great time. All of this while I was pursuing my career.

My co-workers didn't know my personal life and it drove them up the wall. As far as I was concerned, it was none of their business. My career progressed. I got promotions and salary increases, which led to bigger and better outings with my son.

After Andre graduated from college, I applied to and was accepted into New York Law School's Evening Division program. Law school took four years to complete. Classes were four nights, Mondays through Thursdays. I generally arrived home around midnight, would be wired from attending class and did not fall asleep until around 1:30 am. Then, I'd be up at 5 am to start the cycle again. By this time, I was living in

Montclair, New Jersey. My study time began Friday evenings and continued all day Saturdays and Sundays.

Looking back, I didn't consider what it took to raise my son—being present for him—his baseball games, his graduations, parent-teacher nights, advising him as he started his career, etc.—along with holding down a demanding Wall Street job and later graduating from law school as my accomplishments. I viewed my promotions as accomplishments, definitely. But those other things? They were not on my radar until the day that I took time to take my personal inventory. Upon doing so, I was like, "Day-yum! Gurrlll, you did all of that???" It felt like the time just whizzed by. Yet, it's all rooted in the reality of my life.

What's your work-life inventory look like? Have you thought about it? For many of you, irrespective of age, I know you've got a lot to pat yourself on the back for. Doing your personal inventory of your accomplishments is challenging. You get so laser-focused on looking ahead professionally that you neglect to take note of your personal strengths, challenges and successes that served to drive your determination.

Use the space provided to write down the strengths and accomplishments you're most proud of. Be sure to include as many things as you can – completing a college degree, giving birth, raising a child, running a successful business, managing your household finances...anything that brought you satisfaction and joy.

Take your time. Block out time on your calendar for "Me Downtime." Have a comfort drink (i.e., wine, tea, Starbucks coffee, etc.) or object such as a pillow or stuffed toy nearby.

As you begin to write, go in chronological order. There will likely be some efforts you forgot about. Include personal as well as professional successes. Include those times where you needed to take a step back, regroup and move forward. Be non-judgmental. When you're done, read over what you've written. Pat yourself on the back. Celebrate. Offer a toast to yourself.

_____

_____

_____

_____

_____   "I have the opportunity
                                             to begin or continue an
_____   inner journey that can
                                             last the rest of my life."
_____

_____

_____

_____

_____

_____

_____

_____

_____

_____

_____

_____

_____

_____

_____

_____

_____

_____

_____

_____

_____

_____

_____

_____

_____

_____

_____

_____

As you move forward continue to recognize your professional and personal accomplishments to add to your narrative. Your narrative will become a never-ending story because it's how we as women move in the world.

"I want to find out who I am
and give up letting everyone else
define me."

— JUDITH

The 3rd Habit for Reclaiming Your Inner Spirit

Be Present for yourself 24/7

B eing present for yourself requires being willing to tune into your bodily rhythms. One important rhythm that women especially omit to tune into is breathing. Your breath and the mechanism of breathing are connected to your overall wellness. Breathing involves your heart, your lungs and your 5 senses. Your breath feeds your body's operations 24/7. Stress affects your breathing. It causes you to take in less air. It also may cause you to hyperventilate which can result in you becoming light-headed. You can easily feel off balance. You may have to sit down. Your brain is getting insufficient air. Your blood pressure may spike up. Sometimes, insufficient air can stop you in your tracks. Think of those times where you had to stop walking just to catch your breath. Or maybe it's those times when you start tapping your chest or fanning yourself with your hand and say, "Chile, they gonna make me hurt somebody up in here!"

In 2020, the COVID-19 pandemic introduced a heavy layer of stress for all of us. In mid-March 2020, many businesses told their employees to work from home. We all had to scramble to establish a home workspace, shift to virtual meetings and quickly learn the nuances of technology. When we were forced to shelter in place, we had to learn how to be indoors 24/7 with a spouse, partner, children, pets, and maybe other family members. This especially challenged those living in small spaces. Add to that having to wear face masks, limiting the days you go to the grocery store or just go out for air. Some of us, like myself, wore rubber gloves so not to touch anything with my bare hands. Let's not forget that we now had to wash our hands constantly and use hand sanitizer.

With hair and nail salons closed, Black women who are used to having those services done regularly had to cease and desist. For myself, I had to wash and condition my relaxed hair. As it grew, I had to deal with what I called my "hybrid hair" – half permed, combined with new growth. Not fun. I ordered wigs and curly hair. During those early months of the pandemic, I had some creative approaches to hair styles, especially for my work-related virtual calls. I was able to get Box braids done in July by a salon that was fortunate to have already set up socially-distant stations and adopted extensive sanitizing practices.

In late March I was blessed to stumble upon a daily Zoom series that was taught by Saidia Murphy, a Chicago-based African-American yoga teacher and breathwork specialist. Saidia's sessions, which she conducted at 6:30 am (Eastern Time) daily, were right on time. In her sessions, I learned that it's not just enough to breathe. Rather, I learned about the importance of knowing the mechanics of breathing to help lower stress, get centered, and support my overall wellness.

By April, Saidia and her cousin, Azizi Blissett partnered to offer their "Self-Care Rehab Series." Beginning in early April until mid-August, I dialed into their series. Saidia led the participants through 30 minutes of breathwork exercises. Azizi, who is a certified life-coach, facilitated activities that had each participant tap into ourselves, journal our feelings and check our emotional temperatures daily.

Meanwhile, the coronavirus pandemic was raging. I lost friends and acquaintances and that impacted me emotionally. In addition, Azizi lost her brother, with whom both she and Saidia were very close. Having the Self-Care Rehab cohort helped us grieve together. We wrapped up the series with a glorious painting party led by one of the participants.

I share this because I was not fully tuned into the extent of the stress that I took on due to the pandemic and the shelter in place restrictions. Through it all, our employers expected us to still suit up, show up and be present. Granted, many organizations had support services that employees could take advantage of. However, that may not have been enough for women, especially African-American women, faced with job uncertainty, reduced income, remote learning for their children, food insecurity and possibly being caretakers for family members. Then there were the events taking place in the media: the Trump administration's indifference and ignorance about the coronavirus threat, Ahmaud Arbery's murder for jogging-while-Black,

George Floyd's murder, Black Lives Matter demonstrations, the constant media reporting of rising COVID-19 cases and deaths, to name a few.

At the writing of this book, the stress levels are still real. As the likelihood of remote working permanently or some hybrid thereof is at the top of everyone's minds, other concerns are triggered. For example, how and when schools will reopen and whether to allow your child to go back. Getting the extra gear needed to do so. Whether the building owners where you work plan to invest to upgrade their HVAC systems aligned with CDC guidelines. How many days will you be required to be in the office? Will you get vaccinated? So many unanswered questions continue to add to our normal level of stress.

There are a host of subtle stresses that you slog through daily without realizing you're doing so. It's not just the microaggressions and unconscious biases that trigger the stresses. It could be that you're asked to re-do a report. Maybe you've been tasked with an urgent project that was not on your To-Do list for the day. The White person who approaches you in the store because they think you work there. Or the white person who believes face masks violate their First Amendment right and stand a little too close to you on purpose. That unexpected bill or tax payment – you get where I'm going with this. All of these impact your breathing and your mood. From the Self-Care Rehab experience, I learned that allowing yourself to Stop, Breathe, Reset is how you can foster being present for yourself 24/7.

Try this. Become aware of your breathing rhythms during the day. As you consciously tune in to your breathing rhythms, you'll discover how much less air you take in when we you are faced with a stressful situation. Be aware of whether your breathing rhythm increases or becomes shallow as you're listening to the news or while on social media. If so, turn the devices off. It's all right to cut short a telephone conversation with a relative or friend if they're just talking about people, places or situations that are irrelevant to you. While on a WebEx or Zoom call for work, turn off your video if you need to regroup. Take 3 deep breaths before re-engaging. Doing this will help prevent you from possibly overreacting and saying something you may later regret. Find an online meditation session (preferably free), download an app that has soothing sounds, like Calm, that you can listen to.

I urge you to find an outlet to help you breathe and de-stress. Tuning into your breath and your breathing is central to how you tune into yourself, your emotions, your day and ultimately, reclaiming yourself and your inner spirit.

Try this...

In the moment: Pause before reacting. Inhale deeply through your nose. Exhale slowly through your mouth. Do this 3 times. It will help you refocus and re-set your overall demeanor. You can also do this subtly so that others are unaware that you're resetting your breathing.

Connect Inward: As you engage your breathing, mentally scan your body to identify where tension is concentrated: shoulders, neck, jaw, hands, etc. Direct your breath to that area. Visualize your inhalation as cool, calm bright light. Exhale the tension.

Step Away: If you are able to, step away from the situation. Stretch, take a short walk, continue to breathe. If you're in your car, turn your station to classical music, cool jazz, soothing R&B or just turn it off and rest in silence for a moment.

During the day, carve out 5-10 minutes to relax your body and give thanks for the gift of life. Spend some nurturing moments breathing quietly the breath of life, surrounding your body with light. Tune into your honest feelings about your day. Be honest about whether you brought some of the stress on yourself. If so, forgive yourself. Take a deep breath and, as you exhale, say "I love and accept myself." Repeat this 3-4 times. As you continue to adopt this breathing in the moment technique, you'll begin to shift to being present for yourself 24/7.

Use the space below to write down how you felt after doing your breathing in the moment techniques. Do you feel lighter? Were you able to release unwanted tension from your body? Did the experience create a sense of calm and peace within?

_____
_____
_____
_____
_____
_____
_____
_____
_____
_____
_____
_____
_____
_____
_____
_____
_____
_____

"I am fully present and focused. A calm inner peace fills my soul."

Lydia Payne-Johnson

"I can be a wife, a mother,
a lover, a writer – only if I
can be me . . . I exist without
these roles"

— Doris Colona Travis[6]

The 4th Habit for Reclaiming Your Inner Spirit

Express your feelings through writing

Daily journaling is like writing a letter to yourself each day. It is an effective way to release, especially during high stress periods. Getting your feelings on paper can be much better than talking to a friend. Don't stress about writing pages and pages. Some days, you may write no more than 2-3 sentences. It's OK.

Run towards and embrace your feelings. Let your feelings out. Holding in stress and worry can impact your health physically, mentally and emotionally. Holding in your feelings can also result in them manifesting as anger, inappropriate comments, depression, withdrawal, mindless eating, and other unhealthy indulgences that show up against family, friends and co-workers. As you write, you'll see your current mindset come to life on paper. To paraphrase a Yoruba saying,

"[S]he who knows does not die like [S]he who does not know."

I mentioned earlier that journaling was a component of the Self-Care Rehab that I attended last year. We wrote morning pages which became the unedited, uncensored brain dump daily of what was going on inside of me. We also did truth journaling that allowed me an opportunity to express my truth whether it was something I viewed as good, bad or indifferent. I'm amazed when I find notebooks and journals of my writing over the years. Sure, I missed days, even months where I didn't journal. There were times that I was so outwardly focused that I didn't carve out time to get in touch with my feelings.

I recall participating in a group called Tres Dias back in the late 90's. I not only had to journal daily, I also had called a Tres Dias partner daily to read and discuss what I wrote. My recollection is that deep seated feelings came up on occasion. One such memory was my feelings of loneliness and feeling abandoned following my mother's untimely death when I was a senior in college. I also missed having her present to share my successes, to watch my son grow, to hear her laughter and her spirited love for her family. Journaling was a way for me to write and stay connected to her. I also remember writing a scathing set of pages when one of my relationships ended. It was cathartic to unload those feelings on paper and not have to carry them around inside. When we hold onto emotions like that, we open ourselves up to stresses that may manifest as anger, alcoholism, overeating, road rage, depression. These emotions, although rooted in personal issues, will show up in some form or fashion in our performance in the workplace. Your colleagues will notice.

Journaling can help you prioritize your personal and professional goals. It becomes a channel to help you discern the people, places and situations that are assisting you in achieving your goals or distracting you. Importantly, you need to know when to pivot and take an alternative approach. And, most significantly, journaling will be the place where you affirm your wins, your successes, your accomplishments, your milestones – so you can take time to celebrate.

Dedicate a notebook, journal or set up a Word file on your laptop where you capture your thoughts and feelings. Nothing is off limits. Write to yourself.

Use the space below to write yourself. Give yourself permission to express whatever you may be feeling on the inside. Try not to censor yourself. Allow yourself to freely write whatever is coming up for you. Pay attention to how you feel after taking time to journal your thoughts on paper. Do you feel lighter? Has your mood improved any?

_____

_____

_____

_____   *"I own my emotions so*

_____   *that they don't own me."*

_____

_____

_____

_____

_____

_____

_____

_____

Lydia Payne-Johnson

Lydia Payne-Johnson

"When women take care of their health, they become their own best friend".

— MAYA ANGELOU

The 5th Habit for Reclaiming Your Inner Spirit

Become your own best friend

B eing your own best friend allows you to put all of the habits into practice. It means loving yourself. Before getting out of bed in the morning, express gratitude for opening your eyes, hug yourself and say, "I completely love and accept myself." Honor yourself and enjoy who you are.

I am my own best friend when I play the piano. It's one of my passions and it's my stress buster. I've always loved music and dance. Staying active is also another way I am my own best friend. I love being outside. Running and walking are my go-tos during the summer and fall months. Accepting myself requires holding the mirror up to myself.

I never really thought of myself as pretty and so I avoided looking in the mirror as much as possible in my early years. I didn't want to see the "fluffy" parts of my body. I didn't like the shape of my thighs (I now refer to them as my "thigh-roids"). I avoided trying on clothes because I didn't want to see myself in the dressing room mirror. I even avoided looking at myself even on those days when my outfit, hair, nails, makeup were off the chart. Getting to the point of seeing myself, warts and all took a bit of work – as well as the willingness to do the work. Ladies, it's an important big step to becoming your own best friend. Someone you can depend on. Someone who is there for you 24/7, 365 days. Your coach. Your cheerleader. Your trusted advisor.

Being your own best friend means learning to walk in your own spotlight. Shine the light on yourself. Be the star of your life, your career and your family. Take the helm and walk your own runway. On either side of the runway are the affirmations that you selected for yourself. Be confident. Speak and walk your truth. Embrace your accomplishments and celebrate your role in making them happen. Doing this and practicing the other habits in this book is an important step in creating the life you dreamed of.

Use the space below to list the ways you are a best friend to yourself.

_____

_____

_____

_____

_____

_____

_____

"I am my own best friend."

_____

_____

_____

_____

_____

_____

_____

_____

_____

_____

_____

Lydia Payne-Johnson

Conclusion

Microaggressions and unconscious biases are part of the fabric African-American women face daily. It comes with the territory. However, microaggressions and unconscious biases is not your stuff. It's their stuff. The very person who brought it to you. Trying to prove to your White women counterparts that you have achieved work-life balance is an elusive goal. The work-life balance game belongs to them. As mentioned earlier, African-American women have work-life balanced mastered, hands down. You want to avoid falling for the Okie-doke. When you do, you get blamed for getting angry and taking it out on others. You are the one who gets saddled with the health issues. You're the one who gets passed over for promotions. It's time for you to shift the paradigm.

Take time to practice these 5 habits. Be easy on yourself knowing that this will take some time and effort on your part. Remember, you don't have to do this alone. By all means, seek feedback from people you trust. There's a lot to unpack. As a friend shared with me, African-American women navigating the workplace are "bag ladies." We carry around a lot, in the form of emotional baggage. To help you identify your emotional baggage, you may consider getting a mentor or a life coach to help you unpack and lighten your load.

I want you to acknowledge that you innately have all of the talents and gifts necessary for your success and happiness. I want your spotlight to burn brightly. I want you to recognize when those microaggressions, unconscious biases and "isms" start to take you off your game. And when that occurs, I want you to have the courage to step into your truth by practicing these habits to move forward. If you're reading this book, you've taken the first step. I hope that you find these 5 habits designed to help you reclaim your inner spirit to be a blessing in your life.

Be open to change so that, with every new step, you create a new, even better, loving and happier version of yourself.

Biography

Lydia Payne-Johnson is a Diversity and Inclusion Advocate, Speaker and Author. She is the visionary of the Lydia Payne-Johnson brand and new podcast, "What's On Your Mind?." She has become an advocate for women in the workplace. Specifically, around helping them recognize and address  implicit biases and microaggressions that impact women in various areas of their lives. She is also a champion around helping to un-silence African American women who may feel isolated, unfairly criticized, passed over or ignored. Her purpose is to help talented and skilled women find their voice and embrace their true power in the workplace. She believes it is important for women to embrace all of who they are and what they bring to the table as wives, mothers, career women and caretakers. Her mission and hope are to help Black women exhale and recenter to live healthy and fulfilling lives.

Acknowledgments

Thank you to the women who inspired, influenced, challenged and encouraged me mentally, physically and spiritually: my Mother, Verona White, Pearl Primus, Karen Gibbs, Iyalosha Oseye Mchawi, Dr. Sauda Underwood Smith, Iya Cheryl Williams, and Saidia Murphy.

Thanks to my son, Andre Payne for his love and support and for keeping me focused and on track.

Many thanks to Russ Terry for coaching me through those dark days pre-retirement and being my ever-present cheerleader.

Thanks to Baba Bruce Spencer for being a stern task master.

My heartfelt and deep thanks to Azizi Blissett who turned my vision into a tangible reality, pushing me uphill all the way. This book would not have materialized without your creativity, coaching, incredible patience and partnership.

Endnotes

1 Opinion: Facing both COVID-19 and racism, Black women are carrying a particularly heavy burden," Brandi Jackson, co-founding director of the Institute for Antiracism in Medicine and adjunct professor of psychiatry at Rush Medical Center and Aderonk B. Pederson, a researcher funded by the National Institutes of Health and instructor of psychiatry at Northwestern University Feinberg School of Medicine. Both are Public Voices fellows. (*The Washington Post, Opinions*, September 4, 2020)

2 Ibid.

3 *For Colored Girls Who Have Considered Suicide/When the Rainbow is Enuf (New York: Macmillan, 1976)*

4 "12 Powers: Spiritual Tools for an Abundant Life," Unity. https://www.unity.org/resources/twelve-powers

5 "Take Ten, The Adult Timeout for the Creative Soul," Cynthia and Miles Chauvin (2012)

6 "Pardon Me While I Be Myself," Doris Colona Travis (New York: Vantage Press Inc., 1986)

Resources

Anne Wilson Schaef, *"Meditations for Women Who Do Too Much"* (1996)

Iyanla Vanzant, *"Every Day I Pray, Prayers for Awakening to the Grace of Inner Communion"* (2002)

Cynthia Chauvin, Miles Chauvin, *"Take Ten: The Adult Timeout for the Creative Soul"* (2012)

Mark Nepo, *"The Book of Awakening"* (2020)

Panache Desai, *"Discovering Your Soul Signature: A 33-Day Path to Purpose, Passion & Joy"* (2014)

Made in the USA
Monee, IL
13 June 2022

97945460R00049